Fundamental Alexis de Tocqueville:

A Practical Guide to Democracy in America

By M. James Ziccardi

Fundamental Alexis de Tocqueville:

A Practical Guide to Democracy in America

Copyright © 2011 by M. James Ziccardi

All Rights Reserved

ISBN-13: 978-1466330450

ISBN-10: 1466330457

Table of Contents

Preface

This book is one of a series that have been extracted in its entirety from M. James Ziccardi's *Fundamentals of Western Philosophy*.

It is intended to serve as a primer for students of political philosophy and especially Tocqueville's masterpiece, *Democracy in America*.

Notes on the Text

Square brackets [] found within quotes are mine.

Sections in **bold type** or that are <u>underlined</u> are intended by me to highlight critical points.

Alexis de Tocqueville: Background

(1805-1859)

The last of the great political thinkers to be discussed is French-born Alexis de Tocqueville, and the work we will be reviewing is his famous *Democracy in America*: a work that is often regarded as the greatest book ever written on the subject of democracy. Born to a wealthy aristocratic family in Normandy, Tocqueville spent his formative years studying law in Paris, and it was there that he met his life-long friend and future travelling companion, Gustave de Beaumont. In 1831, Tocqueville and Beaumont received a Royal Commission from King Louis-Philippe to travel to America for the purpose of studying its prison systems. Their celebrated expedition lasted just under a year, from May, 1831 to February, 1832, and took them from New England to New Orleans, and as far west as Lake Michigan. The two also spent a brief period of time in Canada.

During their travels, Tocqueville and Beaumont observed and wrote not only about America's prison systems, but about virtually all aspects of American society, including its cultural, religious, economic, and political institutions. For this reason, *Democracy in America* is revered not only for its insights into the American form of democracy, but for its historical insights as well. Tocqueville published *Democracy in America* in two volumes (the first in 1835, and the second in 1840), both of which were quickly well-received and praised for their revealing look into the American experience. (Included in the list of its immediate admirers was John Stuart Mill.)

It is important to note that *Democracy in America* was not written for the American reader, but rather for the members of the French government. At the time of its writing, the concept of self-governance was beginning to spread across Continental Europe, and with it came many questions and concerns about how it would eventually take root there. The self-governance that was beginning to take hold in Europe, however, was fundamentally different from that which existed in America. This is because America had been founded on a codified set of democratic principles that were written into its very constitution. Europe, on the other hand, had nothing of the kind. Consequently, Europe's form of self-governance seemed to be moving on its own accord and without any real structural guidance; after all, the governments of Continental Europe were, for the most part, still in the hands of monarchs.

Tocqueville, who was greatly influenced by the political writings of Jean-Jacques Rousseau (as well as by those of the French philosophers Montesquieu and Blaise Pascal), did not approach democracy with a blank slate, but neither did he approach it with any optimistic preconceived ideas. Instead, he approached democracy knowing it to be an absolute certainty for France, and that the only thing left to be determined was how it would manifest itself. Would it take on a milder form, such as it did in America; or would it be violent and despotic, as it was after the French Revolution?

Tocqueville maintained that the fate of America is the fate of Europe, and quite possibly, the fate of the rest of the world as well. Nonetheless, he believed democracy to be based on the particular political, economic, and social circumstances that are unique to each country, and that therefore, there is no single, or universal, form of democracy that can be applied equally to all countries.

In fact, all countries are, or have the potential to be, different in their implementations of democracy.

Due to its great size, and because it is filled with many technical details concerning the structure and administration of the American government at all its levels, I will not be providing a complete chapter-by-chapter review of this work. Instead, I will be focusing primarily on the judgments, attitudes, and political views that Tocqueville gathered while on his journey across America. Also, in an effort to eliminate any misinterpretations of the text, I have chosen to use Tocqueville's own words as much as possible. With that, the following is a collection of some of the more significant ideas that Tocqueville puts forth in the masterpiece that is *Democracy in America.*

Democracy in America (Volume 1)

In Volume 1, Tocqueville concerns himself chiefly with the implementation and administration of the institutions that go to form the basis of the American democratic government.

Book 1:

Introduction:

1. "Men are not corrupted by the exercise of power or debased by the habit of obedience, but by the exercise of a power which they believe to be illegal and by obedience to a rule which they consider to be usurped and oppressive."
2. "Liberty cannot be established without morality, nor morality without faith."
3. The Church (in Europe) espouses that all men are equal in the eyes of God, and that all are equal in the eyes of the law, but because The Church is so closely tied to those institutions that "democracy assails", i.e., monarchical government, it is not infrequently "brought to reject the equality it loves."

From Chapter 2 – Origin of the Anglo-Americans (Part 1)

1. With respect to the relationship between the early American colonists and the English, "the tie of language is perhaps the strongest and most durable that can unite mankind."
2. "The doctrine of the sovereignty of the people had been introduced into the bosom of the monarchy of the House of Tudor." (This was the

dynasty that included the likes of Henry VIII and Elizabeth I of England.)

3. The original emigrants to the New World were all "men of poverty and misfortune"; therefore, they had no "general notion of superiority over one another."

4. The land in America was not conducive to "territorial aristocracy". Because of this, land was "broken into small portions, which the proprietor cultivated for himself."

5. "Landed property handed down from generation to generation" is the basis of aristocracy and the means by which it is continued.

6. "Slavery...dishonors labor; it introduces idleness into society, and with idleness, ignorance, and pride, luxury and distress. The influence of slavery, united to the English character, explains the manners and the social condition of the Southern States."

7. "The civilization of New England has been like a beacon lit upon a hill, which, after it has diffused its warmth around, tinges the distant horizon with its glow."

8. Regarding the colonies of New England: "A democracy, more perfect than any which antiquity had dreamt of, started in full size and panoply (i.e., magnificence) from the midst of an ancient feudal society."

From Chapter 2 – Origin of the Anglo-Americans (Part 2)

1. England encouraged emigration to America, for it "removed the elements of fresh discord and of further revolutions."

2. "In America...it may be said that the township was organized before the county, the county before the State, the State before the Union."
3. "In America religion is the road to knowledge, and the observance of the divine laws leads men to civil freedom."
4. "Religion is no less the companion of liberty in all its battles and its triumphs, the cradle of its infancy, and the divine source of its claims. The safeguard of morality is religion, and morality is the best security of laws and the surest pledge of freedom."
5. "In America it is the poor who make the law, and they usually reserve the greatest social advantage to themselves."
6. "The surface of American society is...covered with a layer of democracy, from beneath which the old aristocratic colors sometimes seep."

From Chapter 3 – Social Conditions of the Anglo-Americans

1. The "law of entail [i.e., the law of inheritance], unites, draws together, and vests property and power in a few hands: its tendency is clearly aristocratic", the opposite of which "divides, distributes, and disposes both property and power."
2. Under the law of inheritance, property, and especially landed property, "must have a tendency to perpetually diminish." This is because it constantly has to be divided amongst the heirs. This, tendency, therefore, destroys once great families and reduces them to the "general masses."

From Chapter 3 – Political Consequences of the Social Condition of the Anglo-Americans

Here, Tocqueville predicts that American democracy will probably fail. This is because "there exists in the human heart a depraved taste for equality, which impels the weak to attempt to lower the powerful to their own level, and reduces men to prefer equality in slavery to inequality with freedom."

From Chapter 5 – Necessity of Examining the Condition of the States (Part 1)

1. "A nation may establish a system of free government, but without the spirit of municipal institutions it cannot have the spirit of liberty." (By *municipal*, Tocqueville is referring to those institutions which are local and independent.)
2. "Everyone is the best and the sole judge of his own private interest, and that society has no right to control a man's actions, unless they are prejudicial to the [commonwealth], or unless the [commonwealth] demands his cooperation."
3. "Patriotism is not durable in a conquered nation. The New Englander is attached to his township, not only because he was born in it, but because it constitutes a social body of which he is a member, and whose government claims and deserves the exercise of his sagacity."
4. "The revolution of the United States was the result of a mature and dignified taste for freedom, and not a vague or ill-defined craving for independence. It contracted no alliance with the turbulent passions of anarchy; but its course was marked, on the contrary, by an attachment to whatever was lawful and orderly."

5. "It was never assumed in the United States that the citizen of a free country has a right to do whatever he pleases; on the contrary, social obligations were there imposed upon him more various than anywhere else. No idea was ever entertained of attacking the principles or of contesting the rights of society; but the exercise of its authority was divided, to the end that the office might be powerful and the officer insignificant, and that the community should be at once regulated and free. In no country in the world does the law hold so absolute a language as in America, and in no country is the right of applying it vested in so many hands." As such, "the power [in the United States] exists, but its representative is not to be perceived."

From Chapter 5 – Necessity of Examining the Condition of the States (Part 3)

1. "I cannot conceive that a nation can enjoy a secure or prosperous existence without a powerful centralization of government. But I am of the opinion that a central administration enervates the nations in which it exists by incessantly diminishing their public spirit."

2. A centralized government "may contribute admirably to the transient greatness of men, but it cannot ensure the durable prosperity of a nation."

3. In the United States, "the social power is constantly changing hands, because it is subordinate to the power of the people, which is too apt to forget the maxims of wisdom and of foresight in the consciousness of its strength:

hence arises its danger; and will probably be the cause of its ultimate destruction."

4. The government directs the affairs of each locality better than the citizens could do for themselves only "when the central power is enlightened, and when the local districts are ignorant; when it is alert as they are slow; when it is accustomed to act, and they to obey... But I deny that such is the case when the people is as enlightened, as awake to its interests, and as accustomed to reflect on them, as the Americans are. I am persuaded, on the contrary, that in this case the collective strength of the citizens will always conduce more efficaciously to the public welfare than the authority of the government."

5. **"However enlightened and however skilful a central power may be, it cannot of itself embrace all the details of the existence of a great nation. Such vigilance exceeds the powers of man."**

6. In referring to America: "In no country in the world do the citizens make such exertions for the [commonwealth]; and I am acquainted with no people which has established schools as numerous and efficacious, places of public worship better suited to the wants of the inhabitants, or roads kept in better repair."

7. "The end of a good government is to ensure the welfare of a people, and not to establish order and regularity in the midst of its misery and distress."

8. "It profits me but little, after all, that a vigilant authority should protect the tranquility of my pleasures and constantly avert all dangers from

my path, without my care or my concern, if this same authority is the absolute mistress of my liberty and of my life, and if it so monopolizes all the energies of existence that when it languishes everything languishes around it, that when it sleeps everything must sleep, that when it dies the State itself must perish."

9. In a centralized government in which there is little or no local authority, the citizen sees his surroundings as "the property of a powerful stranger whom he calls the government. He has only a life-interest is these possessions, and he entertains no notions of ownership or improvement."

10. "Patriotism and religion are the only two motives in the world which can permanently direct the whole of a body politic to one end."

11. "In America it may be said that no one renders obedience to man, but to justice and law."

12. "As the administrative authority is within the reach of the citizens...it excites neither their jealousy nor their hatred; as its resources are limited, everyone feels that he must not rely solely on its [the government's] assistance."

13. In the United States, "the magistrates and public prosecutors are not numerous, and the examinations of prisoners are rapid and oral. Nevertheless, in no country does crime more rarely elude punishment. The reason is that everyone conceives himself to be interested in furnishing evidence of the act committed, and in stopping the delinquent." Unlike in Europe, where "the population is merely a spectator of the conflict, in America (the criminal) is looked at

as an enemy of the human race, and the whole of mankind is against him."

14. The danger inherent in democracy is that it may descend into despotism of the majority. "In this manner popularity may be conciliated with hostility to the rights of the people, and the secret slave of tyranny may be the professed admirer of freedom."

15. "The only nations which deny the utility of provincial liberties are those which have fewest of them; in other words, those who are unacquainted with the institutions are the only persons who pass a censure upon it."

From Chapter 6 – Judicial Power in the United States

1. "The Americans have acknowledged the right of the judges to found their decisions on the constitution rather than the laws. In other words, they have left (the judges) at liberty not to apply such laws as may appear to them to be unconstitutional."

2. "An American constitution is not supposed to be immutable as in France, nor is it susceptible of modification by the ordinary powers of society as in England."

3. A constitution that undergoes perpetual change "does not in reality exist."

4. In America the constitution may vary according to established rules, "but as long as it exists, it is the origin of all authority, and the sole vehicle of the predominating force."

5. "It is better to grant the power of changing the constitution of the people to men who represent [however imperfectly] the will of the people, than to men who represent no one but themselves."

6. The American judge "only judges the law because he is obliged to judge a case. It is true that upon this system the judicial censorship which is exercised by the courts of justice over the legislation cannot extend to all laws indiscriminately, inasmuch as some of them can never give rise to that exact species of contestation which is termed a lawsuit; and even when such a contestation is possible, it may happen that no one cares to bring it before a court of justice... Within these limits the power vested in the American courts of justice of pronouncing a statute to be unconstitutional forms one of the most powerful barriers which has ever been devised against the tyranny of political assemblies."

From Chapter 7 – Political Jurisdiction in the United States

1. "The principle object of the political tribunals of Europe is to punish the offender; the purpose of those in America is to remove him from authority... The consequence is that in Europe political tribunals are invested with rights which they are afraid to use, and that the fear of punishing too much hinders them from punishing at all. But in America no one hesitates to inflict a penalty from which humanity does not recoil... But this sentence, which is so easy to pronounce, is not the less fatally severe to the majority of those whom it is inflicted. Great criminals may undoubtedly brave its intangible rigor, but ordinary citizens will dread it as a condemnation which destroys their position in

the world, casts a blight upon their honor, and condemns them to a shameful inactivity worse than death."

2. "By preventing political tribunals from inflicting judicial punishments, the Americans seem to have eluded the worst consequences of legislative tyranny, rather than tyranny itself; and I am not sure that political jurisdiction, as it is constituted in the United States, is not the most formidable weapon which has ever been placed in the rude grasp of a of a popular majority." (A case in point to this argument is the impeachment of President Andrew Johnson, who was impeached for no other reason than to have him removed from office.)

From Chapter 8 – The Federal Constitution

1. With regard to the American Revolution, "Separated from their enemies by three thousand miles of ocean, and backed by a powerful ally, the success of the United States may be more justly attributed to their geographical position than to the valor of their armies or to the patriotism of their citizens."

2. Regarding the separation of State and Federal powers, "the attributes of the Federal Government were therefore carefully enumerated and all that was not included amongst them was declared to constitute a part of the privileges to the several governments of the States. Thus the governments of the States remained the rule, and that of the Confederation became the exception."

3. **"The Federalists [i.e., *The Federalist Papers*] is an excellent book, which ought to be**

familiar to the statesmen of all countries, although it especially concerns America."

On the Executive:

4. "This dependence of the executive power [on the legislative power] is one of the defects inherent in republican constitutions."
5. "There is no country in the world in which everything can be provided for by the laws, or in which political institutions can prove a substitute for common sense and public morality."
6. "The authority of the King in France has, in the first place, the advantage of duration over that of the [United States] President, and durability is one of the chief elements of strength; nothing is either loved or feared but what is likely to endure." However, the supremacy of public opinion is above them both. In America, public opinion is exercised "by election and decree; in France it proceeds by revolutions." Therefore, "France with its King is nearer akin to a republic than the Union with its President is to a monarchy."
7. "Several Presidents of the United States have been known to lose the majority in the legislative body without being obliged to abandon the supreme power, and without inflicting a serious evil upon society. I have heard this fact quoted as an instance of the independence and the power of the executive government in America: a moment's reflection will convince us, on the contrary, that it is a proof of its extreme weakness."
8. "No citizen has shown any disposition to expose his honor and his life in order to become the

President of the United States; because the power of that office is temporary, limited, and subordinate."

9. "In elective states...the wheels of government cease to act, as it were, of their own accord at the approach of an election, and even for some time previous to that event."

10. "At the approach of an election the head of the executive government is wholly occupied by the coming struggle; his future plans are doubtful; he can undertake nothing new, and he will only prosecute with indifference those designs which another will perhaps terminate." However, "in the United States the actions of the government may be slackened with impunity, because it is always weak and circumscribed."

11. "One of the principle vices of the elective system is that it always introduces a certain degree of instability into the internal and external policy of the State. But this disadvantage is less sensibly felt if the power vested in the elected magistrate is small."

12. Since it is the prerogative of every American President to replace all of his predecessor's functionaries (which is commonly the case): "to substitute one system for another, as is done in America every four years, by law, is to cause a sort of revolution." For Tocqueville, this is another one of the "evils" of elective government.

On the Mode of Election:

13. "[Political]) parties are strongly interested in gaining the election, not so much with a view to the triumph of their principles under the auspices

of the President-Elect as to show by the majority which returned him, the strength of the supporters of those principles."

On the Re-Election of the President:

14. "Intrigue and corruption are the natural defects of elective government; but when the head of State can be re-elected these evils rise to a great height, and compromise the very existence of the country." This is because "the chief magistrate...borrows the strength of the government for his own purposes." As such, "all laws and all the negotiations he undertakes are to him nothing more than electioneering schemes."

15. "It is impossible to consider the ordinary course of affairs in the United States without perceiving that the desire of being re-elected is the chief aim of the President; that his whole administration, and even his most indifferent measures, tend to this object; and that, as the crisis (election) approaches, his personal interest takes the place of his interest in the public good."

On the Federal Courts:

16. "Governments have in general but two means of overcoming the opposition of the people they govern: the physical force which is at their own disposal, and the moral force which they derive from the decisions of the courts of justice."

17. "A government which should have no other means of exacting obedience than open war must be very near its ruin."

18. "The great end of justice is to substitute the notion of right for that of violence, and to place a legal barrier between the power of the government and the use of physical force."

19. "A federal government stands in greater need of the support of judicial institutions than any other, because it is naturally weak and exposed to formidable opposition."

20. "In America the real strength of the country is vested in the provincial far more than in the Federal Government."

From Chapter 8 – The Federal Constitution (Part 4)

1. With regard to the United States Supreme Court, "a more imposing judicial power was never constituted by any people."

2. The seven justices (as there were at the time of Tocqueville's writing) of the United States Supreme Court "are the all-powerful guardians of a people which respects law, but they would be impotent against popular neglect or popular contempt. The force of public opinion is the most intractable of agents, because its exact limits cannot be defined; and it is not less dangerous to exceed than to remain below the boundary prescribed."

3. Unlike the President or the United States Congress, "if the Supreme Court is ever composed of imprudent men or bad citizens, the Union may be plunged into anarchy or civil war."

4. "The existence of democracies is threatened by two dangers: the complete subjection of the legislative body to the caprices of the electoral body, and the concentration of all the powers of the Government in the legislative authority."

5. Unlike America's first constitution of 1781, the *Articles of Confederation and Perpetual Union*, "the American States which combined in 1789 (though ratified in 1788) agreed that the Federal Government should not only dictate the laws, but that it (rather than the States) should execute its own enactments... This alteration produced the most momentous consequences." This "novel theory" is to be regarded as "a great invention in modern political science", for by this theory the subordination of the States was made possible.

6. "In America the subjects of the Union are not the States, but private citizens: the national Government levies a tax, not upon the State of Massachusetts, but upon each inhabitant of Massachusetts. All former confederate governments presided over communities, but that of the Union rules individuals; its force is not borrowed, but self-derived; and it is served by its own civil and military officers, by its own army, and its own courts of justice." Therefore, in America "the Federal Government has the means of enforcing all it is empowered to demand."

From Chapter 8 – The Federal Constitution (Part 5)

1. Generally speaking, "in small nations there are more persons in easy circumstances, a more numerous population, and a more tranquil state of society, than in great empires." This is because is small nations, "all the efforts and resources of the citizens are turned to the internal benefit of the community, and are not likely to evaporate in the fleeting breath of glory."

2. "Small nations have therefore ever been the cradle of political liberty; and the fact that many of them have lost their immunities by extending their dominion shows that the freedom they enjoyed was more a consequence of the inferior size than of the character of the people."

3. "The history of the world affords no instance of a great nation retaining the form of republican government for a long series of years, and this has led to the conclusion that such a state of things is impracticable." Tocqueville disagrees with this conclusion, but he admits that "the existence of a great republic will always be exposed to far greater perils than of a small one."

4. "All the passions which are fatal to republican institutions spread with an increasing territory."

5. "The ambition of the citizens increases with the power of the State."

6. "It may therefore be asserted as a general proposition that nothing is more opposed to the well-being and the freedom of man than vast empires."

7. "If none but small nations existed, I do not doubt that mankind would be more happy and more free; but the existence of great nations is unavoidable."

8. **With regard to "the element of physical strength as a condition of national prosperity,…it profits a people but little to be affluent and free if it is perpetually exposed to be pillaged and subjugated; the number of its manufacturers and the extent of its commerce are of small advantage if another**

nation has the empire of the seas and gives the law in all the markets of the globe."

9. "Small nations are often impoverished, not because they are small, but because they are weak; the great empires prosper less because they are great than because they are strong. Physical strength is therefore one of the first conditions of the happiness and even the existence of nations."

10. "Hence it occurs that, unless very peculiar circumstances intervene, small nations are always united to large empires in the end, either by force or by their own consent: yet I am unacquainted with a more deplorable spectacle than that of a people unable either to defend or maintain its independence."

11. "The confederation of all the American States presents none of the ordinary disadvantages resulting from great agglomerations [masses] of men. The Union is a great republic in extent, but the paucity [fewness] of objects for which its Government provided assimilates it to a small State."

12. "The Union is as happy and as free as a small people, and as glorious and as strong as a great nation."

13. "The governments which are founded upon a single principle or a single feeling which is easily defined and perhaps not the best...are unquestionably the strongest and the most durable in the world."

14. **"The Constitution of the United States...is the most perfect federal constitution that ever existed", yet "one is startled...at the variety of information and the excellence of**

discretion which it presupposes in the people whom it is meant to govern. The government of the Union depends entirely upon legal fictions; the Union is an ideal nation which only exists in the mind, and whose limits and extent can only be discerned by the understanding."

15. "The whole structure of the [American] Government is artificial and conventional; and it would be ill adapted to a people which has not been long accustomed to conduct its own affairs, or to one in which the science of politics has not descended to the humblest classes of society. I have never been more struck by the good sense and practical judgment of the Americans than in the ingenious devices by which they elude the numberless difficulties resulting from their Federal Constitution."

16. **"All the people which have ever formed a confederation have been held together by a certain number of common interests, which served as the intellectual ties of association."**

17. "One of the circumstances which most powerfully contribute to support the Federal Government in America is that the States have not only similar interests, a common origin, and a common tongue, but that they are also arrived at the same stage of civilization; which almost always renders a union feasible."

18. "I cannot believe that any confederate peoples could maintain a long or an equal contest [war] with a nation of similar strength in which the government should be centralized. A people [who] should divide its sovereignty into fractional

powers, in the presence of the great military monarchies of Europe, would, in my opinion, by that very act, abdicate its power, and perhaps its existence and its name." (As for the American Revolution, Tocqueville claims that the Union was saved "by the weakness of its enemies far more than by its own strength.")

From Chapter 10 – Parties in the United States

1. "(Political) parties are a necessary evil in free governments."
2. "The political parties which I style great are those which cling to principles more than to their consequences; to general, and not especial cases; to ideas, and not to men."
3. "When the war of Independence was terminated, and the foundations of the new Government were laid down, the nation was divided between two opinions -- two opinions which are as old as the world, and which are perpetually to be met with under all the forms and all the names which have ever obtained in free communities – the one tending to limit, the other to extend indefinitely, the power of the people." These two sentiments form the underlying sentiment of all political parties.
4. As is the nature of political parties, "the prevailing party assumes the credit of having restored peace and unanimity to the country. But this apparent unanimity is merely a cloak to alarming dissensions and perpetual opposition."
5. "The wealthy members of the community entertain a hearty distaste to the democratic institutions of their country. The populace is at once the object of their scorn and of their fears."

6. "The two chief weapons which the parties use in order to ensure success are the public press and the formation of associations."

From Chapter 11 – Liberty of the Press in the United States

1. "The influence of the liberty of the press does not affect political opinions alone, but it extends to all the opinions of men, and it modifies customs as well as laws."
2. Tocqueville does not entertain the notion that the liberty of the press is a "supreme good". Instead, he approves of it "more from a recollection of the evils it prevents than from a consideration of the advantages it ensures."
3. "The language in which a thought is embedded is the mere carcass of the thought, and not the idea itself; tribunals may condemn the form, but the sense and spirit of the work is too subtle for their authority."
4. "If you establish a censorship of the press, the tongue of the public speaker will still make itself heard, and you have only increased the mischief." Thus, to destroy the liberty of the press, "the liberty of discourse must therefore be destroyed as well." And to destroy the liberty of discourse is to be brought "to the feet of a despot."
5. "In countries in which the doctrine of the sovereignty of the people ostensibly prevails, the censorship of the press is not only dangerous, but it is absurd."
6. In America, "it is adopted as an axiom of political science...that the only way to neutralize the

effect of public journals is to multiply them indefinitely."

From Chapter 12 – Political Associations in the United States

1. "The independence of the press...is the chief and, so to speak, the constitutive element of freedom in the modern world. A nation which is determined to remain free is therefore right in demanding the unrestrained exercise of this independence. But the unrestrained liberty of political association cannot be entirely assimilated to the liberty of the press."

2. "There are no countries in which associations are more needed, to prevent the despotism of faction or the arbitrary power of a prince, than those which are democratically constituted."

3. "In countries where associations are free, secret societies are unknown. In America there are numerous factions, but no conspiracies."

4. **"The most natural privilege of man, next to the right of acting for himself, is that of combining his exertions with those of his fellow-creatures, and of acting in common with them. I am therefore led to the conclusion that the right of association is almost as inalienable as the right of personal liberty."**

From Chapter 13 – Government of the Democracy in America (Part 1)

1. "It cannot be denied that democratic institutions have a very strong tendency to promote the feeling of envy in the human heart; not so much

because they afford to everyone the means of rising to the level of any of his fellow-citizens, as because those means perpetually disappoint the persons who employ them. Democratic institutions awaken and foster a passion for equality which they can never entirely satisfy."

2. "The natural propensities of democracy induce the people to reject the most distinguished citizens as its rulers." This is because there is a tendency among the people to resent the superior classes of society.

3. "I hold it to be sufficiently demonstrated that universal suffrage is by no means a guarantee of the wisdom of the popular choice."

4. "In the estimation of the democracy, a government is not a benefit, but a necessary evil."

5. In America, "the public officers themselves are well aware that they only enjoy the superiority over their fellow-citizens which they derive from their authority upon condition of putting themselves on a level with the whole community by their manners. A public officer in the United States is uniformly civil, accessible to all the world, attentive to all requests , and obliging in his replies…and I was struck by the manly independence of the citizens, who respect the office more than the officer, and who are less attached to the emblems of authority than to the man who bears them."

6. "When a democratic republic renders offices which had formally been remunerated (paid) gratuitous, it may safely be believed that the State is advancing to monarchical institutions; and when a monarchy begins to remunerate

such officers as had hitherto been unpaid, it is a sure sign that it is approaching toward a despotic or a republican form of government. The substitution of paid functionaries is of itself, in my opinion, sufficient to constitute a serious revolution."

7. "I look upon the entire absence of gratuitous functionaries in America as one of the most prominent signs of the absolute dominion which democracy exercises in that country."

8. "In nations in which the principle of election extends to every place in the State no political career can, properly speaking, be said to exist." This is because no elected officer can ever be sure of retaining his office.

From Chapter 13 – Government of the Democracy in America (Part 2)

1. "Although a democratic government is founded upon a very simple and natural principle, it always presupposes the existence of a high degree of culture and enlightenment in society. At the first glance it may be imagined to belong to the earliest ages of the world; but maturer observation will convince us that it could only come last in the succession of human history."

2. "The government of the middle classes appears to me to be the most economical, though perhaps not the most enlightened, and certainly not the most generous, of free governments."

3. **When the legislative authority "is vested in the lowest orders...the tendency of the expenditure will be to increase, not to diminish. As the great majority of those who create the laws are possessed of no property**

upon which taxes can be imposed, all the money which is spent for the community appears to be spent to their advantage, at no cost of their own; and those who are possessed of some little property readily find means of regulating the taxes so that they are burdensome to the wealthy and profitable to the poor."

4. "The government of the democracy is the only one under which the power which lays on taxes escapes the payment of them."

5. "Universal suffrage [because it includes the poor] does therefore, in point of fact, invest the poor with the government of society."

From Chapter 13 – Government of the Democracy in America (Part 3)

1. "In aristocratic governments the individuals who are placed at the head of affairs are rich men, who are solely desirous of power. In democracies statesmen are poor, and they have their fortunes to make. The consequence is that in aristocratic States the rulers are rarely accessible to corruption, and have very little craving for money; whilst the reverse is the case in democratic nations. In the United States I never heard a man accused of spending his wealth in corrupting the populace; but I have often heard the probity [integrity] of public officers questioned; still more frequently have I heard their success attributed to low intrigues and immoral practices."

2. "I am of opinion that a democratic government tends in the end to increase the real strength of society; but it can never combine, upon a single

point and at a given time, so much power as an aristocracy or a monarchy."

3. "As for myself I have no hesitation in avowing my conviction, that it is most especially in the conduct of foreign relations that democratic governments appear to me to be decidedly inferior to governments carried on upon different principles."   Furthermore, "good sense may suffice to direct the ordinary course of society…but such is not always the case in the mutual relations of foreign nations."

From Chapter 14 – Advantages American Society Derive From Democracy (Part 1)

1. "Aristocracies are infinitely more expert in the science of legislation than democracies ever can be. They are possessed of a self-control which protects them from the errors of temporary excitement, and they form lasting designs which they mature with the assistance of favorable opportunities. Aristocratic government proceeds with the dexterity of art… Such is not the case with democracies, whose laws are almost always ineffective or inopportune. The means of democracy are therefore more imperfect than those in aristocracy, and the measures which it unwittingly adopts are frequently opposed to its own cause."

2. "The great advantage of the Americans consists in their being able to commit faults which they may afterward repair."

3. "I say that it is important that the interests of the persons in authority should not conflict with or oppose the interests of the community at large; but I do not insist upon their having the same

interests as the whole population, because I am not aware that such a state of things ever existed in any country."

4. "No political form has hitherto been discovered which is equally favorable to the prosperity and the development of all the classes into which society is divided… The advantage of democracy does not consist, therefore…in favoring the prosperity of all, but simply in contributing to the well-being of the greatest possible number."

5. "The men who are entrusted with the direction of public affairs in the United States are frequently inferior, both in point of capacity and of morality, to those whom aristocratic institutions would raise to power. But their interest is identified and confounded with that of the majority of their fellow-citizens. They may frequently be faithless and frequently mistaken, but they will never systematically adopt a line of conduct opposed to the will of the majority; and it is impossible that they should give a dangerous or an exclusive tendency to the government."

6. "The most powerful, and perhaps the only, means of interesting men in the welfare of their country…is to make them partakers in the government", as is the case in the United States.

7. "If…you do not succeed in connecting the notion of rights with that of personal interest, what means will you have of governing the world except by fear?"

From Chapter 14 – Advantages American Society Derive From Democracy (Part 2)

1. "The people in America obeys the law not only because it emanates from the popular authority, but because that authority may modify it in any points which may prove vexatory; a law is observed because it is a self-imposed evil in the first place, and an evil of transient duration in the second."

2. "Democracy does not confer the most skilful kind of government upon the people, but it produces that which the most skilful governments are frequently unable to awaken, namely, an all-pervading and restless activity, a superabundant force, and an energy which is inseparable from it, and which may, under favorable circumstances, beget the most amazing benefits. These are the true advantages of democracy."

3. Democracy is not suited "to confer a certain elevation upon the human mind," or to "teach it to regard the things of this world (such as poetry, beauty, or the renown) with generous feelings". However, "if you are of the opinion that the principle object of a government is not to confer the greatest possible share of power and of glory upon the body of the nation, but to ensure the greatest degree of enjoyment and the least degree of misery to each of the individuals who compose it...you can have no surer means of satisfying them than by equalizing the conditions of men, and establishing democratic institutions."

From Chapter 15 – Unlimited Power of Majority, and Its Consequences (Part 2)

1. "A majority taken collectively may be regarded as a being whose opinions, and most frequently whose interests, are opposed to those of another being, which is styled a minority. If it be admitted that a man, possessing absolute power, may misuse that power by wronging his adversaries, why should a majority not be liable to the same reproach?"

2. "The form of government which is usually termed mixed has always appeared to me to be a mere chimera. Accurately speaking there is no such thing as a mixed government...because in all communities some one principle of action may be discovered which preponderates over the others."

3. "Unlimited power is in itself a bad and dangerous thing: human beings are not competent to exercise it with discretion."

4. "When I see that the right and the means of absolute command are conferred on a people or upon a king, upon an aristocracy or a democracy, a monarchy or a republic, I recognize the germ of tyranny, and I journey onward to a land of more hopeful institutions."

5. "A distinction must be made between tyranny and arbitrary power. Tyranny may be exercised by means of the law, and in that case it is not arbitrary; arbitrary power may be exercised for the goof of the community at large, in which it is not tyrannical. Tyranny usually employs arbitrary means, but, if necessary, it can rule without them."

On the Effects Democracy has on Public Opinion:

6. "It is in the examination of the display of public opinion in the United States that we clearly perceive how far the power of the majority surpasses all the powers with which we are acquainted in Europe."

7. "The authority of a king is purely physical, and it controls the actions of the subject without subduing his private will; but the majority possesses a power which is physical and moral at the same time; it acts upon the will as well as upon the actions of men, and it represses not only all contest, but all controversy. I know no country in which there is so little true independence of mind and freedom of discussion as in America."

8. "In America the majority raises very formidable barriers to the liberty of opinion: within these barriers an author may write whatever he pleases, but he will repent it if he ever [steps] beyond them."

9. "If great writers have not at present existed in America, the reason is very simply given in these facts; there can be no literary genius without freedom of opinion, and freedom of opinion does not exist in America. The Inquisition has never been able to prevent a vast number of anti-religious books from circulating in Spain. The empire of the majority succeeds much better in the United States, since it actually removes the wish of publishing them."

On the Dangers of Unlimited Power of the Majority:

10. "I am persuaded that in all governments, whatever their nature may be, servility will cower to force, and adulation will cling to power. The only means of preventing men from degrading themselves is to invest no one with that unlimited authority which is the surest method of debasing them."

11. "It is almost always by the abuse of its force and the misemployment of its resources that a democratic government fails."

12. **"If ever the free institutions of America are destroyed, that event may be attributed to the unlimited authority of the majority, which may at some future time urge the minorities to desperation, and oblige them to have recourse to physical force. Anarchy will then be the result, but it will have been brought about by despotism."** Here, Tocqueville points out that Alexander Hamilton makes the same assertion in *The Federalist Papers, No. 51.* (*Federalist No. 51* was written by James Madison in 1788.) Tocqueville further points out that Thomas Jefferson makes the same case in a letter to Madison. (It is worth noting that Tocqueville considered Jefferson to be "the most powerful advocate democracy has ever sent forth.")

From Chapter 16 – Causes Mitigating Tyranny in the United States (Part 1)

On Lawyers:

1. **"If a democratic republic similar to that of the United States were ever founded in a country where the power of a single individual had previously subsisted, and the effect of a centralized administration had sunk so deep into the habits and the laws of the people, I do not hesitate to assert, that in that country a more insufferable despotism would prevail than any which now exists in the monarchical States of Europe, or indeed any which could be found on this side of the confines of Asia."**

2. "The authority (that the Americans) have entrusted to members of the legal profession, and the influence which these individuals exercise in the Government, is the most powerful existing security against the excesses of democracy."

3. "The object of lawyers is not, indeed to overthrow the institutions of democracy, but they constantly endeavor to give it an impulse which diverts it from its real tendency, by means which are foreign to its nature."

4. "I question whether democratic institutions could long be maintained, and I cannot believe that a republic could subsist at the present time if the influence of lawyers in public business did not increase in proportion to the power of the people."

5. "The English and the Americans have retained the law of precedents; that is to say, they

continue to found their legal opinions and the decisions of their courts upon the opinions and the decisions of their forefathers. In the mind of an English or American lawyer a taste and a reverence for what it old is almost always united to a love of regular and lawful proceedings."

6. If there is an American aristocracy, then "it occupies the judicial bench and the bar."

From Chapter 16 – Causes Mitigating Tyranny in the United States (Part 2)

On Juries:

1. "The jury is above all, a political institution, and it must be regarded in this light in order to be duly appreciated."

2. "The true sanction of political laws is to be found in penal legislation, and if that sanction be wanting the law will sooner or later lose its cogency. He who punishes infractions of the law is therefore the real master of society… The institution of the jury consequently invests the people, or that class of citizens, with the direction of society."

3. "The system of the jury, as it is understood in America, appears to me to be as direct and as extreme a consequence of the sovereignty of the people as universal suffrage. These institutions are two instruments of equal power, which contribute to the supremacy of the majority."

4. "The jury, and more especially the jury in civil cases, serves to communicate the spirits of the judges to the minds of all the citizens; and this

spirit, with the habits which attend it, is the soundest preparation for free institutions."

5. "The jury contributes most powerfully to form the judgment and to increase the natural intelligence of a people, and this is, in my opinion, its greatest advantage."

6. In civil cases, as opposed to criminal ones, "it is the judge who sums up the various arguments with which (the jurors) memory has been wearied out, and who guides them through the devious course of the proceedings; he points their attention to the exact question of fact which they are called upon to solve, and he puts the answer to the question of law into their mouths. His influence upon their verdict is almost unlimited."

7. **In civil cases, "whenever the question to be solved is not a mere question of fact, the jury has only the semblance of a judicial body. The jury sanctions the decision of the judge, they by the authority of society which they represent, and he by that of reason and of law."**

From Chapter 17 – Principle Causes Maintaining the Democratic Republic (Part 2)

1. The three circumstances which contribute most powerfully to the maintenance of the democratic republic (of the United States) are:
   a. The federal form of government, "which enables the Union to combine the power of a great empire with the security of a small State."
   b. The municipal institutions, "which limit the despotism of the majority, and at the same

time impart a taste for freedom and a knowledge of the art of being free to the people."

c. The "constitution of the judicial power."

Also contributing to the maintenance of a democratic republic are the social mores, or what Tocqueville calls "the manners" of the people.

On Religion:

2. The Catholics "constitute the most republican and the most democratic class of citizens which exist in the United States." (It should be noted that Tocqueville was a Catholic.)

3. "I think that the Catholic religion has erroneously been looked upon as the natural enemy of democracy. Amongst the various sects of Christians, Catholicism seems to me, on the contrary, to be one of those which are most favorable to the equality of conditions. In the Catholic Church, the religious community is composed of only two elements, the priest and the people. The priest alone rises above the rank of his flock, and all below him are equal."

4. Unlike Catholicism, "Protestantism…generally tends to make men independent, more than to render them equal."

5. "In the United States religion exercises but little influence upon the laws and upon the details of public opinion, but it directs the manners of the community, and by regulating domestic life it regulates the State."

6. "Religion is often unable to restrain man from the numberless temptations of fortune…but its

influence over the mind of woman is supreme, and women are the protectors of morals."

7. "Whilst the law permits the Americans to do what they please, religion prevents them from conceiving, and forbids them to commit, what is rash or unjust."

8. "I do not know whether all the Americans have a sincere faith in their religion, for who can search the human heart? But I am certain that they hold it to be indispensable to the maintenance of republican institutions. This opinion is not peculiar to a class of citizens or to a party, but it belongs to the whole nation, and to every rank of society."

9. "Despotism may govern without faith, but liberty cannot."

From Chapter 17 – Principle Causes Maintaining the Democratic Republic (Part 3)

1. Contrary to the predictions of the philosophers of the eighteenth century who believed that religious faith would necessarily fail "the more generally liberty is established and knowledge diffused", in America "one of the freest and most enlightened nations in the world fulfils all the outward duties of religious fervor."

2. "Religion…is simply another form of hope; and it is no less natural to the human heart than hope itself."

3. "Unbelief is an accident, and faith is the only permanent state of mankind."

4. "If the unbeliever does not admit religion to be true, he still considers it useful."

From Chapter 17 – Principle Causes Maintaining the Democratic Republic (Part 4)

1. "There are...no nations upon the face of the earth more miserable than those in South America...Physical causes do not, therefore, affect the destiny of nations so much as has been supposed."

2. "The laws [and especially] the manners of the Anglo-Americans are therefore that efficient cause of their greatness which is the cause of my inquiry."

3. **With regard to the fact that several of the South American countries had modeled their laws and constitutions after those of the United States: "The manners of the Americans of the United States are, then, the real cause which renders that people the only one of the American nations that is able to support a democratic government; and it is the influence of manners which produces the different degrees of order and of prosperity that may be distinguished in the several Anglo-American democracies [i.e., the individual American States[."**

4. For Tocqueville, the three things most important to the maintenance of a democratic republic are (in order of their importance): its manners, its legislation, and its geographical position.

5. By the example of America, it is shown "that laws, and especially manners, may exist which will allow a democratic people to remain free. But I am very far from thinking that we ought to follow the example of American democracy, and copy the means which it has employed to attain

its ends; for I am well aware of the influence which the nature of a country has and its precedents exercise upon a constitution; and I should regard it as a great misfortune for mankind if liberty were to exist all over the world under the same forms."

From Chapter 18 – Future Conditions of the Three Races in the United States (Part 2)

1. Regarding the treatment and conditions of the America Indians: "These are great evils; and it must be added that they appear to me to be irremediable. I believe that the Indian Nations of North America are doomed to perish; and that whenever the Europeans shall be established on the shores of the Pacific Ocean, that race of men will be no more."

2. "The Indians had only the two alternatives of war or civilization; in other words, they must either have destroyed the Europeans or became their equals.

From Chapter 18 – Future Conditions of the Three Races in the United States (Part 3)

1. According to Tocqueville, "it is not for the good of the negroes, but for that of the whites, that measures are taken to abolish slavery in the United States."

2. "The colonies in which there were no slaves became more populous and more rich than those in which slavery flourished. The more progress was made, the more was it shown that slavery, which is so cruel to the slave, is prejudicial to the master." This is because in

States in which slavery exists, labor is degraded; but in those in which it does not, labor is honored.

From Chapter 18 – Future Conditions of the Three Races in the United States (Part 4)

1. "The free workman is paid, but he does his work quicker than the slave, and rapidity of execution is one of the great elements of economy."

2. "The money which a master spends in the maintenance of his slaves goes gradually and in detail, so that it is scarcely perceived; the salary of the free workman is paid in a round sum, which appears only to enrich the individual who receives it, but in the end the slave has cost more than the free servant, and his labor is less productive."

3. One of the primary reasons for the predominance of slavery in the South was the "law of primogeniture". This law established that only the eldest son of a wealthy land owner could inherit the family estate, which meant that his younger brothers remained in the "same state of idleness as their elder brother, without being as rich... This aristocracy contained many who were poor, but none who would work; its members preferred want to labor, consequently no competition was set on foot against negro laborers and slaves." (Eventually, however, when this law was abolished, all heirs -- who were then able to inherit equal but small shares of the estate for their own subsistence -- were reduced to accept a state of labor. This is turn established a competition of labor between the free workmen and the slaves, from which it

became manifest that the labor of the latter was inferior to that of the former, at least with respect to the interests of the master.)

From Chapter 18 – Future Conditions of the Three Races in the United States (Part 5)

1. "As soon as it is admitted that the whites and the emancipated blacks are placed upon the same territory in the situation of two alien communities, it will readily be understood that there are but two alternatives for the future; the negroes and the whites must either wholly part or wholly mingle [through interracial marriage]... I do not imagine that the white and black races will ever live in any country upon an equal footing." Here, Tocqueville offers a quote from the Memoirs of Jefferson (by M. Conseil) that echoes the same sentiment: "Nothing is more clearly written in the book of destiny than the emancipation of the blacks; and it is equally certain, that the two races will never live in a state of equal freedom under the same government, so insurmountable are the barriers which nature, habit, and opinion have established between them." It is obvious that both man failed to envision the day in which all backs would not only be free citizens, but that they would come to hold the highest offices in the land.

2. "God forbid that I should seek to justify the principle of negro slavery, as has been done by some American writers! But I only observe that all the countries which formally adopted that execrable principle are not equally able to abandon it at the present time."

3. "The events which are taking place in the Southern States of the Union appear to me to be at once the most horrible and the most natural results of slavery. When I see the order of nature overthrown, and when I hear the cry of humanity in its vain struggle against the laws, my indignation does not light upon the men of our own time who are the instruments of these outrages, but I reserve my execration for those who, after a thousand years of freedom, brought back slavery into the world once more."

From Chapter 18 – Future Conditions of the Three Races in the United States (Part 6)

1. "It appears to me unquestionable that if any portion of the Union seriously desired to separate itself from the other States, they would not be able, nor indeed would they attempt, to prevent it; and that the present Union will only last as long as the States which compose it choose to continue [to be] members of the confederation. If this point be admitted, the question becomes less difficult; and our object is, not to inquire whether the States of the existing Union are capable of separating, but whether they will choose to remain united." Here again, Tocqueville failed to recognize the destructive consequences that slavery, both directly and indirectly, would eventually bring upon the Union and lead to civil war, as well as the degree to which the Union would fight to preserve itself.

Democracy in America (Volume 2)

Book 2: Influences of Democracy on Progress of Opinion in the United States

Section 1: Influence of Democracy on the Action of Intellect in the United States

From Chapter 1 - Philosophical Method Among the Americans

1. "I think that in no country in the civilized world is less attention paid to philosophy than in the United States. The Americans have no philosophical school of their own; and they care but little for all the schools into which Europe is divided, the very names of which are scarcely known to them." Nonetheless, there is "a philosophic method of the Americans... America is therefore one of the countries in the world where philosophy is least studied, and where the percepts of Descartes are best applied." (It should be noted that about thirty-five years after Tocqueville made these remarks, the uniquely American philosophic discipline of *pragmatism* began to emerge. *American Pragmatism*, as it is more commonly referred to, was founded on the *pragmatic maxim* that was put forth by the American philosopher Charles Sanders Peirce in 1878. At its core, Peirce's maxim deals with finding the optimal way of "attaining clearness of apprehension".)

2. "The Americans then have not (been) required to extract their philosophic method from books;

they have found it in themselves." This is in part because the social condition of the Americans "deters them from speculative studies."

From Chapter 2 - Of the Principle Source of Belief Among Democratic Nations

1. "In order that society should exist...and prosper, it is required that all the minds of the citizens should be rallied and held together by certain predominant ideas; and this cannot be the case, unless each of them sometimes draws his opinions from the common source, and consents to accept certain matters of belief at the hands of the community."

2. In democracies, the equality of conditions "leads men to entertain a sort of instinctive incredulity of the supernatural, and a very lofty and often exaggerated opinion of human understanding... They commonly seek for the sources of truth in themselves, or in those who are like themselves." For this reason, it is difficult, if not impossible, for new religions to be established under these conditions.

3. When conditions of inequality exist, as is the case in aristocracies, the opinions of the masses are more easily shaped by those they consider to be their intellectual superiors. However, when men live under conditions of equality, they are less prone "to place implicit faith in a certain man or a certain class of men, but they are more prone to believe in the common opinions of the multitude." In other words, they see that "the greater truth should go with the greater number."

4. "When the inhabitant of a democratic country compares himself individually with all those

about him, he feels with pride that he is the equal of any one of them; but when he comes to survey the totality of his fellows, and to place himself in contrast to so huge a body, he is instantly overwhelmed by the sense of his own insignificance and weakness." For this reason, public opinion is essentially forced into the minds of a democratic people, whereas in an aristocracy, it is merely persuaded.

From Chapter 3 - Why the Americans Display More Readiness and More Taste for General Ideas Than Their Forefathers, the English

1. "Men who live in ages of equality have a great deal of curiosity and very little leisure; their life is so practical, so confused, so excited, so active, that but little time remains to them for thought." As such, men of democracies "are prone to general ideas because they spare them the trouble of studying particulars." (Here, Tocqueville uses the term *general ideas* to refer to *abstract ideas*, which are the concepts we apply to whole classes of objects rather than to individual, or *particular*, objects.)

From Chapter 5 - Of the Manner In Which Religion In the United States Avails Itself of Democratic Tendencies

1. "Fixed ideas of God and human nature are indispensible to the daily practice of men's lives; but the practice of their lives prevents them from acquiring such ideas."
2. "The first object and one of the principle advantages of religions, is to furnish to each of [the] fundamental questions a solution which is

at once clear, precise, intelligible to the mass of mankind, and lasting." Even religions which are "very false and very absurd" may be conducive to man's happiness, provided they do not hinder "the free progress of man's mind."

3. "When the religion of a people is destroyed, doubt gets hold of the highest portions of the intellect, and half paralyzes all the rest of its powers... Such a condition cannot but enervate the soul, relax the springs of the will, and prepare a people for servitude." For this reason, Tocqueville doubts "whether man can ever support at the same time complete religious independence and entire public freedom."

4. The greatest advantage of religion, however, is that it places "the object of man's desires above and beyond the treasures of the earth", and raises his soul "to regions far above those of the senses." Furthermore, religion imposes a sense of duty on man; and since this is contrary to the democratic nature, it is important for men to "preserve their religion as their conditions become more equal."

5. **Religions ought to "confine themselves within their own precincts; for in seeking to extend their power beyond religions matters, they incur a risk of not being believed at all." In this regard, the human intellect "should be left in entire freedom to its own guidance." Tocqueville points out that unlike the Gospel, "which only speaks of the general relations of men to God and to each other", the Koran is not only "a body of religious doctrines", but also a body of "political maxims, civil and criminal law, and theories**

of science." For Tocqueville, "this alone, besides a thousand other reasons, would suffice to prove that (Islam) will never long predominate in a cultivated and democratic age, whilst [Christianity] is destined to retain its sway at these as at all other periods."

6. During periods of equality, religion should not attempt to completely control or eradicate man's love of riches. Instead, it should "persuade men to enrich themselves by none but honest means."

7. "The more the conditions of men are equalized and assimilated to each other, the more important it is for religions...not needlessly to run counter to the ideas which generally prevail, and the permanent interests which exist in the mass of the people."

From Chapter 8: The Principle of Equality Suggests to the Americans the Idea of the Indefinite Perfectibility of Man

1. Of all the animals, man is the only one that is capable of improvement; and since mankind "could not fail to discover this difference from its earliest period", this notion is therefore "as old as the world."

2. "Aristocratic nations are naturally too apt to narrow the scope of human perfectibility; democratic nations, to expand it beyond reason."

From Chapter 9 - The Examples of the Americans Does Not Prove that a Democratic People Can Have No Aptitude and No Taste for Science, Literature, or Art

1. "It must be acknowledged that amongst few of the civilized nations of our time have the higher sciences made less progress than in the United States; and in few have great artists, fine poets, or celebrated writers been more rare." This is due in part by the American form of worship, which is "hostile to external symbols and to ceremonial pomp", both of which are "naturally favorable to the fine arts, and only yields a reluctant sufferance to the pleasures of literature." The other reason for this lack of prevalence in the arts and sciences is because in America, "everyone finds facilities, unknown elsewhere, for making or increasing his fortune. The spirit of gain is always on the stretch, and the human mind, constantly diverted from the pleasures of imagination and the labors of the intellect, is there swayed by no impulse but the pursuit of wealth." Therefore, the deficiency of science and art in the United States is not due to democratic principles in general, but rather to the form of democracy that is "only American".

2. "When men living in a democratic state of society are enlightened, they readily discover that they are confined and fixed within no limits which constrain them to take up with their present fortune. They all therefore conceive the idea of increasing it; if they are free, they all attempt it, but all do not succeed in the same manner."

3. **"As natural inequality is very great, fortunes become unequal as soon as every man exerts all his facilities to get rich."**

4. "The inequality of fortunes augments in proportion as knowledge is diffused and liberty increased."

5. "Natural inequality will very soon make way for itself, and wealth will spontaneously pass into the hands of the most capable."

6. **"When heredity wealth, the privileges of rank, and the prerogatives of birth have ceased to be, and when every man derives his strength from himself alone, it becomes evident that the chief cause of disparity between the fortunes of men is the mind."**

From Chapter 10 - Why the Americans Are More Addicted to Practical than to Theoretical Science

1. "The permanent inequality of conditions [as is the case in aristocracies] leads men to confine themselves to the arrogant and sterile research of abstract truths; whilst the social conditions and the institutions of democracy prepare them to seek the immediate and useful practical results of the sciences. This tendency is natural and inevitable."

2. "With education and freedom, men living in democratic ages cannot fail to improve the industrial part of science."

From Chapter 20 - Characteristics of Historians in Democratic Ages

1. In general, historians in democratic societies attribute events to general causes, while those

in aristocratic societies attribute them to the special influences of certain individuals. Furthermore, historians in democracies tend to find connections between events and then deduce systems from them, while those in aristocracies find no such connections and tend to treat events as isolated incidents.

2. The danger for the historians of democratic societies is that because they fail (at least in part) to attribute the causes of events to individuals, they often see that the movement of history "is involuntary, and that societies unconsciously obey some superior force ruling over them." This in turn may lead mankind to the mistaken belief that they have no free will of their own.

3. "In reading the historians of aristocratic ages, and especially those of antiquity, it would seem that, to be master of his lot, and to govern his fellow-creatures, man requires only to be master of himself. In perusing the historical volumes which our age has produced, it would seem that man is utterly powerless over himself and over all around him."

4. "The historians of antiquity taught how to command: those of our time teach only how to obey; in their writings the author often appears great, but humanity is always diminutive." (Tocqueville refers to this as the *doctrine of necessity*.)

5. "Our contemporaries are but too prone to doubt of the human free-will, because each of them feels himself confined on every side by his own weakness; but they are still willing to acknowledge the strength and independence of

men united in society. Let not this principle be lost sight of; for the great object in our time is to raise the faculties of men, not to complete their prostration."

Section 2: Influence of Democracy on the Feelings of Americans

From Chapter 1 - Why Democratic Nations Show a More Ardent and Enduring Love of Equality than of Liberty

1. **"The taste which men have for liberty, and that which they feel for equality, are, in fact, two different things; and I am not afraid to add that, amongst democratic nations, they are two unequal things."**
2. "Freedom has appeared in the world at different times and under various forms, and it is not confined to democracies. Freedom cannot, therefore, form the distinguishing characteristic of democratic ages. The peculiar and preponderating fact which marks those ages as its own is the equality of conditions; the ruling passion of men in those periods is the love of this equality."
3. **"None but attentive and clear-sighted men perceive the perils with which equality threatens us, and they commonly avoid pointing them out. They know that the calamities they apprehend are remote, and flatter themselves that they will only fall upon future generations, for which the present generation takes but little thought."**

4. "The evils which freedom sometimes brings with it are immediate; they are apparent to all, and all are more or less affected by them. The evils which extreme equality may produce are slowly disclosed; they creep gradually into the social frame; they are only seen at intervals, and at the moment at which they become most violent, habit already causes them to be no longer felt."

From Chapter 2 - Of Individualism in Democratic Countries"

1. Egoism, or what Tocqueville calls *the passionate and exaggerated love of self*, "originates in blind instinct". Individualism, on the other hand, proceeds from "erroneous judgment more than from depraved feelings; it originates as much in the deficiencies of the mind as in the perversity of the heart." (Tocqueville claims individualism to be of "democratic origin".)
2. In democratic societies, individuals acquire or retain "sufficient education and fortune to satisfy their own wants. They owe nothing to any man, they expect nothing from any man; they acquire the habit of always considering themselves as standing alone, and they are apt to imagine that their whole destiny is in their own hands."

From Chapter 3 - Individualism Stronger at the Cost of a Democratic Revolution than at Other Periods

1. "The great advantage of the Americans is that they have arrived at a state of democracy without having to endure a democratic revolution

(against an aristocracy); and that they are born equal, instead of becoming so."

From Chapter 4: That the Americans Combat the Effects of Individualism by Free Institutions

1. "To combat the evils which equality may produce, there is only one effectual remedy – namely, political freedom."

From Chapter 5 - Of the Use Which the Americans Make of Public Associations in Civil Life

1. **"The morals and the intelligence of a democratic people would be as much endangered as its business and manufactures, if the government ever wholly usurped the place of private companies."**
2. In democratic nations, the circulation of ideas should be done through private associations and not the government, for when the government attempts to do so, "it exercises, even unintentionally, an unsupportable tyranny."
3. "If men are to remain civilized, or to become so, the art of associating together must grow and improve in the same ratio in which the equality of conditions is increased."

From Chapter 8 - The Americans Combat Individualism by the Principle of Interest Rightly Understood

In this chapter, Tocqueville presents his own code of morality, which he calls *the principle of interest rightly understood*.

1. "When the world was managed by a few rich and powerful individuals, these persons loved to

entertain a lofty idea of the duties of man. They were fond of professing that it is praiseworthy to forget one's self, and that good should be done without hope of reward, as it is by the Deity himself... I doubt whether men were more virtuous in aristocratic ages than in others; but they were more incessantly talking of the beauties of virtue, and its utility was only studied in secret." (This is one of the best refutations that can be made to Kant's morality of self-sacrifice; for from a position of high social status, as Kant surely held, it is a cheap virtue to insist that the poor masses of an aristocratic society should sacrifice themselves without any hope of reward.)

2. In more democratic times, moralists "content themselves with inquiring whether the personal advantage of each member of the community does not consist in working for the good of all; and when they have hit upon some point on which private interest and public interest meet and amalgamate, they are eager to bring it into notice...and it is held as a truth that man serves himself in serving his fellow-creatures, and that his private interest is to do good."

3. "The American moralists do not profess that men ought to sacrifice themselves for their fellow-creatures because it is noble to make such sacrifices; but they boldly aver that such sacrifices are as necessary to him who imposes them upon himself as to him for whose sake they are made." For Tocqueville, self-interest is not the egoistical and selfish tendency we usually think of when we hear the term. Rather, it is the "enlightened regard" that individuals

have for themselves which "constantly prompts them to assist each other, and inclines them willingly to sacrifice a portion of their time and property to the welfare of the State." In this sense, what is good for others and the State is also good for the individual. This is what Tocqueville means when he talks about the *principle of interest rightly understood*. For him, this principle is "not a lofty one, but it is clear and sure...and as it lies within the reach of all capacities, everyone can without difficulty apprehend and retain it."

4. "The principle of interest rightly understood produces no great acts of self-sacrifice, but it suggests daily small acts of self-denial. By itself it cannot suffice to make a man virtuous, but it disciplines a number of citizens in habits of regularity, temperance, moderation, foresight, and self-command; and, if it does not lead men straight to virtue by the will, it gradually draws them in that direction by their habits".

5. **"I am not afraid to say that the principle of interest, rightly understood, appears to me the best suited of all philosophical theories to the wants of men in our time, and that I regard it as their chief remaining security against themselves. Towards it, therefore, the minds of the moralists of our age should turn; even should they judge it to be incomplete, it must nevertheless be adopted as necessary."**

From Chapter 12 - Causes of Fanatical Enthusiasm in Some Americans

1. "Religious insanity is very common in the United States." (Tocqueville uses the example of the wandering preachers of the West and their tented revivals to illustrate this point.)
2. "The soul has wants which must be satisfied; and whatever pains be taken to divert it from itself, it soon grows weary, restless, and disquieted amidst the enjoyments of sense."

From Chapter 13 - Causes of the Restless Spirit of Americans in the Midst of Their Prosperity

1. Americans are "forever brooding over advantages they do not possess. It is strange to see with what feverish ardor the Americans pursue their own welfare; and to watch the vague dread that constantly torments them lest they should not have chosen the shortest path to which may lead to it. A native of the United States clings to this world's goods as if he were certain never to die; and he is so hasty in grasping all within his reach, that one would suppose he was constantly afraid of not living long enough to enjoy them. He clutches everything, he holds nothing fast, but soon loosens his grasp to pursue fresh gratifications."
2. **In a near parroting of Plato's description of the democratic soul in Book 8 of *The Republic*, Tocqueville says the following: "In the United States a man builds a house to spend his latter years in it, and he sells it before the roof is on: he plants a garden, and lets it just as the trees are coming into**

bearing: he brings a field into tillage, and leaves other men to gather the crops: he embraces a profession, and gives it up: he settles in a place, which he soon afterwards leaves to carry his changeable longings elsewhere. If his private affairs leave him any leisure, he instantly plunges into the vortex of politics; and if at the end of a year of unremitting labor he finds he has a few day's vacation, his eager curiosity whirls him over the vast extent of the United States, and he will travel fifteen hundred miles in a few days, to shake off his happiness. Death at length overtakes him, but it is before he is weary of his bootless chase of that complete felicity which is forever on the wing."

3. "He who has set his heart exclusively upon the pursuit of worldly welfare is always in a hurry, for he has but a limited time at his disposal to reach it, to grasp it, and to enjoy it. The recollection of the brevity of life is a constant spur to him. Besides the good things which he possesses, he every instant fancies a thousand others which death will prevent him from trying if he does not try them soon. This thought fills him with anxiety, fear, and regret, and keeps his mind in ceaseless trepidation, which leads him perpetually to change his plans and his abode."

4. **"Whatever efforts a people may make, they will never succeed in reducing all the conditions of society to a perfect level; and even if they unhappily attained that absolute and complete depression, the inequality of minds would still remain, which, coming**

directly from the hand of God, will forever escape the laws of man."

5. "The desire of equality always becomes more insatiable in proportion as equality is more complete."

From Chapter 15 - That Religious Belief Sometimes Turns the Thoughts of the Americans to Immaterial Pleasures

1. "The belief in a supersensual or immortal principle, united for a time to matter [as the soul is united to the body], is so indispensible to man's greatness, that its effects are striking even when it is not united to the doctrine of future reward or punishment; and when it holds no more than that after death the divine principle contained in man is absorbed in the Deity, or transferred to animate the frame of some other creature." Therefore, according to Tocqueville, any form of idealism, even if it is in the form of reincarnation, is better for man than pure materialism.

2. Regarding State religions, "I have always held that if they be sometimes of momentary service to the interest of political power, they always, sooner or later, become fatal to the Church."

3. "I believe that the sole effectual means which governments can employ in order to have the doctrine of the immortality of the soul duly respected, is ever to act as if they believed in it themselves; and I think that it is only by scrupulous conformity to religious morality in great affairs that they can hope to teach the community at large to know, to love, and to observe it in the lesser concerns of life."

From Chapter 20 - That Aristocracy May Be Enlightened By Manufactures

1. Manufacturing "lowers the class of workmen; it raises the class of masters."
2. "Whereas the workman concentrates his facilities more and more upon the study of a single detail, the master surveys a more extensive whole, and the mind of the latter is enlarged in proportion as that of the former is narrowed."
3. "The master and the workmen have then here no similarity, and their differences increase every day. They are only connected as the two rings at the extremes of a long chain. Each of them fills the station which is made for him, and out of which he does not get: the one is continually, closely, and necessarily dependent upon the other, and seems as much born to obey as that other is to command. What is this but aristocracy?"
4. "The small aristocratic societies which are formed by some manufacturers in the midst of the immense democracy of our age contain, like the great aristocratic societies of former ages, some men who are very opulent, and a multitude who are wretchedly poor."
5. "I am of opinion, upon the whole, that the manufacturing aristocracy which is growing up under our eyes is one of the harshest which ever existed in the world; but at the same time it is one of the most confined and least dangerous. Nevertheless the friends of democracy should keep their eyes anxiously fixed in this direction; for if ever a permanent inequality of conditions

and aristocracy again penetrate into the world, it may be predicted that this is the channel by which they will enter."

Book 3: Influence of Democracy on Manners, Properly So Called

From Chapter 1 - That Manners Are Softened As Social Conditions Become More Equal

1.   "When all the ranks of a community are nearly equal, as all men think and feel in nearly the same manner, each of them may judge in the moment of the sensations of all the others; he casts a rapid glance upon himself, and that is enough. It signifies not that strangers or foes be the sufferers; imagination puts him in their place; something like a personal feeling is mingled with his pity, and makes himself suffer whilst the body of his fellow-creature is in torture.   In democratic ages men rarely sacrifice themselves for one another; but they display general compassion for the members of the human race. They inflict no useless ills; and they are happy to relieve the griefs of others; when they can do so without much hurting themselves; they are not disinterested, but they are humane."

2.   The "horrid suffering" and "barbarous punishments" of the American slaves demonstrate that the mildness of manners is "attributed to the equality of conditions, rather than to civilization and education."   (In this statement, Tocqueville is stating that manners tend to be mild only when they are practiced among members of the same social class.)

3. "As nations become more like each other, they become reciprocally more compassionate, and the law of nations is mitigated."

From Chapter 7 - Influence of Democracy on Wages

1. "I think that, upon the whole, it may be asserted that a slow and gradual rise of wages is one of the general laws of democratic communities. In proportion as social conditions become more equal, wages rise; and as wages are higher, social conditions become more equal."

From Chapter 8 - Influence of Democracy on Kindred

1. "I think that, in proportion as manners and laws become more democratic, the relation of father and son becomes more intimate and more affectionate; rules and authority are talked less of, confidences and tenderness are oftentimes increased, and it would seem that the natural bond is drawn closer in proportion as the social bond is loosened. In a democratic family the father exercises no other power than that with which men love to invest the affection and the experience of age; his orders would perhaps be disobeyed, but his advice is for the most part authoritative." In other words, "the master and the constituted ruler have vanished – the father remains."
2. "Democracy loosens social ties, but it draws the ties of nature more tight; it brings kindred more closely together, whilst it places the various members of the community more widely apart."

From Chapter 12 - How the Americans Understand the Equality of the Sexes

1. "It may readily be conceived, that by...attempting to make one sex equal to the other, both are degraded; and from so preposterous a medley of the works of nature nothing could ever result but weak men and disorderly women."
2. "The Americans have applied to the sexes the great principle of political economy which governs the manufactures of our age, by carefully dividing the duties of men from those of women, in order that the great work of society may be the better carried out."
3. "The Americans do not think that man and woman have either the duty or the right to perform the same offices, but they show an equal regard for both their respective parts; and though their lot is different, they consider both of them as being of equal value."

From Chapter 13 - That the Principle of Equality Naturally Divides the Americans Into a Number of Small Private Circles

1. **"Whatever may be the general endeavor of a community to render its members equal and alike, the personal pride of individuals will always seek to rise above the line, and to form somewhere an inequality to their own advantage."**

From Chapter 18 - Of Honor in the United States and In Democratic Communities

1. For Tocqueville, honor "is a system of opinions peculiar to themselves as to what is blamable or commendable; and these peculiar rules always originate in the special habits and special interests of the community." In other words, what is considered to be honorable in one community or class may not necessarily be considered as such in another.

2. The condition in the United States is "that of an almost exclusively manufacturing and commercial association... This is the characteristic which most peculiarly distinguishes the American people from all others at the present time. All those quiet virtues which tend to give a regular movement to the community, and to encourage business, will therefore be held in peculiar honor by that people, and to neglect those virtues will be to incur public contempt." (Here, Tocqueville is referring only to those Americans "inhabiting those States where slavery does not exist", since for him, these alone "can be said to present a complete picture of democratic society.")

3. In the United State, "where fortunes are scanty and insecure, everybody works, and work opens a way to everything: this has changed the point of honor quite around, and has turned it against idleness." This is in direct contradiction to the aristocratic societies of Europe. There, any labor that is necessary for one's subsistence is considered to be dishonorable, while idleness,

on the other hand, is considered to be honorable.

4. "Amongst a democratic nation, like the Americans, in which ranks are confounded and the whole of society forms one single mass, composed of elements which are all analogous though not entirely similar, it is impossible ever to agree beforehand on what shall or shall not be allowed by the law of honor."

5. "As honor, amongst democratic nations, is imperfectly defined, its influence is of course less powerful; for it is difficult to apply with certainty and firmness a law which is not distinctly known."

From Chapter 19 - Why So Many Ambitious Men and So Little Lofty Ambition are to be Found in the United States

1. "The principle of equality, which allows every man to arrive at everything, prevents all men from rapid advancement." This is due to a rise in competition which naturally proceeds from the principle of equality; and it is this competition which leads to the lack of ambition, or at least the ambition of a higher degree, that is seen in democratic societies. The danger with this is that a diminished sense of ambition often tends to slow "the march of society".

From Chapter 20 - The Trade of Pace-Hunting In Certain Democratic Countries

1. **"When public employments are few in number, ill-paid and precarious, whilst the different lines of business are numerous and lucrative, it is to business, and not to official**

duties, that the new and eager desires engendered by the principle of equality turn from every side. But if, whilst the ranks of society are becoming more equal, the education of the people remains incomplete, or their spirit the reverse of bold – if commerce and industry, checked in their growth, afford only slow and arduous means of making a fortune – the various members of the community, despairing of ameliorating their own condition, rush to the head of the State and demand its assistance. To relieve their own necessities at the cost of the public treasury, appears to them to be the easiest and most open, if not the only, way they have to rise above a condition which no longer contents them." Tocqueville refers to this as *place-hunting*, and he considers it to be "a great social evil". This is because it "destroys the spirit of independence in the citizens, and diffuses a venal and servile humor throughout the frame of society." Furthermore, "this kind of traffic only creates an unproductive activity, which agitates the country without adding to its resources."

2. "A government which encourages this tendency (place-hunting) risks its own tranquility, and places its very existence in great jeopardy."

3. "When public employments afford the only outlet for ambition, the government necessarily meets with a permanent opposition at last; for it is tasked to satisfy with limited means unlimited desires." A safer and more honest course of action is for

the sovereigns to teach their subjects "the art of providing for themselves."

From Chapter 21 - Why Great Revolutions Will Become More Rare

1. "In democratic communities, the majority of the people [i.e., the middle class] do not clearly see what they have to gain by a revolution, but they continually and in a thousand ways feel that they might lose by one."
2. "I know of nothing more opposite to revolutionary manners than commercial manners."
3. "Nations are less disposed to make revolutions in proportion as personal property is augmented and distributed amongst them, and as the number of those possessing it increases."
4. "Violent political passions have but little hold on those who have devoted all their faculties to the pursuit of their well-being."
5. **"From time to time indeed, enterprising and ambitious men will arise in democratic communities, whose unbound aspirations cannot be contented by following the beaten track. Such men like revolutions and hail their approach; but they have great difficulty in bringing them about, unless unwonted events come to their assistance. No man can struggle with advantage against the spirit of his age and country; and however powerful he may be supposed to be, he will find it difficult to make his contemporaries share in feelings and opinions which are repugnant to all their feelings and desires." Such a man "strains himself to rouse the**

indifferent and distracted multitude, and finds at last that he is reduced to impotence, not because he is conquered, but because he is alone."

6. "Men living in democratic communities...love change, but they dread revolution."

From Chapter 22 - Why Democratic Nations Are Naturally Desirous of Peace, and Democratic Armies of War

1. "I speak no ill of war: war almost always enlarges the mind of a people, and raises their character. In some cases it is the only check to the excessive growth of certain propensities which naturally spring out of the equality of conditions, and it must be considered as a necessary corrective to certain inveterate diseases to which democratic communities are liable."

2. "There are two things which a democratic people will always find very difficult – to begin a war, and to end it."

3. "No protracted war can fail to endanger the freedom of a democratic country... War does not always give over democratic communities to military government, but it must invariably and immeasurably increase the powers of civil government." Consequently, "all those who seek to destroy the liberties of a democratic nation ought to know that war is the surest and the shortest means to accomplish it. This is the first axiom of the science." For Tocqueville, the primary danger of war lies not in defeat or in any resulting military government, but rather in the increase of power to the exiting government.

From Chapter 26 - Some Considerations on War in Democratic Communities

1. "When the principle of equality is in growth, not only amongst a single nation, but amongst several nations at the same time, as is now the case in Europe, the inhabitants of these different countries, notwithstanding the dissimilarity of language, of customs, and of laws, nevertheless resemble each other in their equal dread of war and their common love of peace."

2. Because the interests of nations that share in the principle of equality "are so mixed and entangled with one another...no nation can inflict evils on other nations without those evils falling back upon itself; and all nations ultimately regard war as a calamity, almost as severe to the conqueror as to the conquered."

3. **"It is extremely difficult in democratic ages to draw nations into hostilities; but on the other hand, it is impossible that any two of them should go to war without embroiling the rest."**

4. In sovereign and independent democratic nations, "civil wars will become much less frequent and less protracted." In democratic confederacies (such as the United States), however, "civil wars are in fact nothing but foreign wars in disguise."

Book 4: Influence of Democratic Opinions on Political Society

From Chapter 2: That the Notions of Democratic Nations on Government are Naturally Favorable to the Concentration of Power

1. "The Americans hold, that in every State the supreme power ought to emanate from the people; but when once that power is constituted, they can conceive, as it were, no limits to it, and they are ready to admit that it has the right to do whatever it pleases."

From Chapter 3 - That the Sentiments of Democratic Nations Accord With Their Opinions in Leading Them to Concentrate Political Power

1. "If it be true that, in ages of equality, men readily adopt the notion of a great central power, it cannot be doubted on the other hand that their habits and sentiments predispose them to recognize such a power and to give it their support."

2. Individuals in democratic societies **"may be willing to admit, as a general principle, that the public authority ought not to interfere in private concerns; but, by an exception to that rule, each of them craves for its assistance in the particular concern on which he is engaged, and seeks to draw upon the influence of the government for his own benefit, though he would restrict it on all other occasions. If a large number of men apply this particular exception to a great variety of different purposes, the sphere of**

the central power extends insensibly in all directions, although each of them wishes it to be circumscribed. Thus a democratic government increases its power simply by the fact of its permanence. Time is on its side; every incident befriends it; the passions of individuals unconsciously promote it; and it may be asserted, that the older a democratic community is, the more centralized will its government become."

3. "Every central power which follows its natural tendencies courts and encourages equality; for equality singularly facilitates, extends, and secures the influence of a central power."

4. "Democratic nations often hate those in whose hands the central power is vested; but they always love that power itself."

5. "I am of opinion, that, in the democratic ages which are opening upon us, individual independence and local liberties will ever be the products of artificial contrivance; that centralization will be the natural form of government."

From Chapter 4 - Of Certain Peculiar and Accidental Causes Which Either Lead a People to Complete Centralization of Government, Or Which Divert Them From It

1. "A revolution which overthrows an ancient regal family, in order to place men of more recent growth at the head of a democratic people, may temporarily weaken the central power, but however anarchical such a revolution may appear at first, we need not hesitate to predict

that its final and certain consequence will be to extend and to secure the prerogatives of that power."

2. **"The foremost or indeed the sole condition which is required in order to succeed in centralizing the supreme power in a democratic community, is to love equality, or to get men to believe you love it. Thus the science of despotism, which was once so complex, is simplified, and reduced as it were to a single principle."**

From Chapter 5 - That Amongst the European Nations of Our Time the Power of Governments is Increasing, Although the Persons Who Govern as Less Stable

1. **"In proportion as the duties of the central power are augmented, the number of public officers by whom that power is represented must increase also. They form a nation in each nation; and as they share the stability of the government, they more and more fill up the place of an aristocracy."**

2. **"Some charitable persons conceive the notion of collecting the savings of the poor and placing them out at interest. In some countries these benevolent associations are still distinct from the State; but in almost all they manifestly tend to identify themselves with the government; and in some of them the government has superseded them, taking upon itself the enormous task of centralizing in one place, and putting out at interest on its own responsibility, the daily savings of many millions of the working classes... Thus the sovereign does not confine himself**

to the management of the public treasury; he interferes in private money matters; he is the superior, and often the master, of all the members of the community; and, in addition to this, he assumes the part of their steward and paymaster."   Because of the people's love of this "welfare", they are placed "in closer dependence upon those who govern", and thus are on the "roads to servitude."

3.   "As a nation becomes more engaged in manufactures, the want of roads, canals, harbors, and other works of a semi-public nature, which facilitate the acquisition of wealth, is more strongly felt; and as a nation becomes more democratic, private individuals are less able, and the State more able, to execute works of such magnitude. I do not hesitate to assert that the manifest tendency of all governments at the present time is to take upon themselves alone the execution of these undertakings; by which means they daily hold in closer dependence the population which they govern."

4.   "As private persons become more powerless by becoming more equal, they can effect nothing in manufactures without combination [i.e., organized labor]; but the government naturally seeks to place these combinations under its own control."

5.   In democratic societies, the manufacturers end up governing the people, and the government ends up governing the manufacturers.

6.   "As long as the democratic revolution was glowing with heat, the men who were bent upon the destruction of old aristocratic

powers hostile to that revolution displayed a strong spirit of independence; but as the victory or the principle of equality became more complete, they gradually surrendered themselves to the propensities natural to that condition of equality, and they strengthened and centralized their governments. They had sought to be free in order to make themselves equal; but in proportion as equality was more established by the aid of freedom, freedom itself was thereby rendered of more difficult attainment."

From Chapter 6 - What Sort of Despotism Democratic Nations Have to Fear

1. "If despotism were to be established amongst the democratic nations of our days...it would become more extensive and more mild; it would degrade men without tormenting them."
2. The principle of equality facilitates despotism.
3. According to Tocqueville, the future state of government in democratic societies, and especially in America, will not be one of despotism or tyranny, but rather one composed of guardians. As such, above a democratic people "stands an immense and tutelary (protective) power, which takes upon itself alone to secure their gratifications, and to watch over their fate. That power is absolute, minute, regular, provident, and mild. It would be like the authority of a parent, if, like that authority, its object was to prepare men for manhood; but it seeks, on

the contrary, to keep them in perpetual childhood." (It seems as though Tocqueville had arrived at the idea of *Big Brother* government more than a century before George Orwell coined the term in his 1949 novel, *Nineteen Eighty-Four*.)

4. With respect to the future happiness of a democratic people, "such a government willingly labors, but it chooses to be the sole agent and the only arbiter of that happiness: it provides for their security, foresees and supplies their necessities, facilitates their pleasures, manages their principle concerns, directs their industry, regulates the descent of property, and subdivides their inheritances – what remains, but to spare them all the care of thinking and all the trouble of living? Thus it every day renders the exercise of the free agency of man less useful and less frequent; it circumscribes the will within a narrower range, and gradually robs a man of all the uses of himself. The principle of equality has prepared men for these things: it has predisposed men to endure them, and oftentimes to look on them as benefits."

5. Under such conditions, "the will of man is not shattered, but softened, bent, and guided: men are seldom forced by it to act, but they are constantly restrained from acting: such a power does not destroy, but it prevents existence; it does not tyrannize, but it compresses, enervates, extinguishes, and stupefies a people, till each nation is reduced to nothing better than a flock of timid and

industrious animals, of which the government is the shepherd." As for the people, they are left to "consol themselves for being in tutelage by the reflection that they have chosen their own guardians."

6. "A great many persons at the present day are quite contented with this sort of compromise between administrative despotism and the sovereignty of the people; and they think they have done enough for the protection of individual freedom when they have surrendered it to the power of the nation at large."

From Chapter 7 - Continuation of the Preceding Chapters

1. "I believe that it is easier to establish an absolute and despotic government amongst a people in which the conditions of society are equal than amongst any other; and I think that if such a government were once established amongst such a people, it not only would oppress men, but would eventually strip each of them of several of the highest qualities of humanity. Despotism therefore appears to me peculiarly to be dreaded in democratic ages. I should have loved freedom, I believe, at all times, but in the time in which we live I am ready to worship it."

2. To thwart the tendencies towards despotism that are naturally inherent in democratic societies, Tocqueville offers the following: democratic societies must endeavor "to lay down extensive but distinct and settled limits to the action of government; to confer certain rights on private persons, and to

secure to them the undisputed enjoyment of those rights; to enable individual man to maintain whatever independence, strength, and original power he still possesses; to raise him by the side of society at large, and uphold him in that position." Furthermore, "it would seem as if the rulers of our time sought only to use men in order to make thinks great; I wish that they would try a little more to make great men; that they would set less value on the work and more upon the workman; that they would never forget that a nation cannot long remain strong when every man belonging to it is individually weak; and that no form or combination of social polity has yet been devised to make an energetic people out of a community of pusillanimous and enfeebled citizens."

From Chapter 8 - General Survey of the Subject

Tocqueville concludes the book with the following observation and warning:

"The nations of our time cannot prevent the conditions of men from becoming equal; but it depends upon themselves whether the principle of equality is to lead them to servitude or freedom, to knowledge or barbarism, to prosperity or wretchedness.

INDEX